poems of the
modern gay boy

"An accurate portrayal of what it means to be alive and gay today."

> — AJ, modern gay boy from New Jersey

"I never realized how relatable my own story was until I read modern gay boy. I love this book, and you will too!"

> — Nic Strazza, modern gay boy from New York

"A wonderfully written representation of the thoughts and feelings of a gay boy growing up in this crazy world."

> — James N, modern gay boy from Pennsylvania

"As a young gay man, this book is touching. It hits home in a way that makes you cry and laugh as you look back at the moments that shaped you into who you are today."

> — Geovanny Fischetti, modern gay boy from New Jersey

Also by Joseph Anthony

An Uneaten Breakfast:
Collected Stories and Poems

"Warm poetry and short stories make a pleasant combination. Captivating—keeps the reader on the edge of his or her chair." —Bea Smith, The Local Source

"Using lyrical poetry and prose, Mr. Anthony adeptly weaves a map of the emotional landscapes within and between his characters. *An Uneaten Breakfast* resides strongly and comfortably among classic and contemporary masterpieces." —Samsara Literary Magazine

The Alphabet of Dating

"Will have you cataloging your own quest for love. Seasoned, crisp…and full of universal truths." —Richard Polk, author of *Mantis Prayers* and *The Boarder on Monroe Street*

"An intriguing tale of the nuance of relationships and the impact they have on us all." —Linda Rawlins, author of *Sacred Gold* and *Fatal Breach*.

"Relevant…Innovative…Highly recommended." —Samsara Literary Magazine

Some College Somewhere

Stories chronicling the life of a self-destructive college student. What would you do if you were alone in the world, at college, and had just under one million dollars?

poems of the

modern
gay
boy

joseph
anthony

published by diamond mill press
184 south livingston avenue suite 9-198
livingston, new jersey 07039

the poem "big gay lottery" was first published june of 2016, appearing in issue 13 of *lavender review*. the poem "epiphany" was first published in june, 2016, appearing in volume five, issue 20 of *the corner club press*. the poems "here's to you," "love is not oil," "fight for you," magic pill," "outlaws," and "we were born," were all selected for publication by *eleventh transmission*. "first kiss" was selected for publication by *heart online*. a version of the poem "the unaccepted" first appeared in joseph anthony's *an uneaten breakfast: collected stories and poems* © 2011. the poem "republicans and democrats" was the winner of the *yellow chair review's* "rock the chair" challenge, the first week of april, 2016.

isbn # 978-0-9838745-7-7
library of congress control number: 2016959889

10 9 8 7 6 5 4 3 2 1

cover design by joseph anthony
cover photo and all other images licensed through shutterstock., inc. all rights reserved to the appropriate copyright holders. images appear in no chronological order: oksanka007, dolly kuzmina, aleksandra, watchara, anna macabre, rayphotographer, mossolainen, nikolai, mrs. opossum, anna vtorykn, anna ismagilova, radiocat, mejnak, nadia x, ritard lemon, tina bits, anna42f, renee reeder bfa, mr. suttipon yakham, evgeniia speshneva, christos georghiou, heidrun gellrich, pressmaster, evannovostro, albert flint, ajakor, fona, kaidash, artem musaev, jet, faenkova elena, studiolondon, mitrushova tatiana, galyna_p, melodist, athalaric, tina bits, chevnenko, evgeny turaev, rommy tod, le panda, Berezina, alohaflaminggo

to the gay boys of the past,
who made life better for the
modern gay boy.

and, to the gay boys
of the future.

in these pages

we are together,

for a brief

few moments.

"Life should be beautiful."

-John Donovan

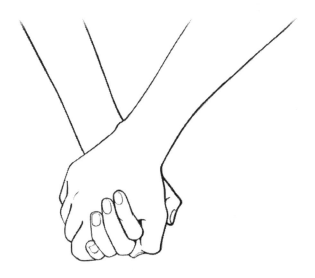

contents

modern gay boy

epiphany

when i was 13, i already knew
i could feel it, and asked: why me of anyone?
of all that this could happen to

for years, the silent struggle of an unnecessary plight
a battle eventually both won and lost
  with   acceptance
      ↕
    self

              it really goes back even further...

                            seven years old, second grade
                    coloring with cody on the reading-rug carpet
                            where we wrote our own story
                                            about
                                a penguin who was lost
                                        and needed
                                to find his way home.

fight for you

i admired you for your bravery.
for having the guts to be yourself
when it wasn't easy.

for taking everyone's shit when you shouldn't have had to
and for not letting them take away that part of you that smiled
and danced.

you didn't know about me.
or maybe you did and chose not to say anything.
for that, i admire you, too.

i remember the first time i saw you
get pushed down by some jerks in the hallway.
they were getting on you for the way you talked
and the way you carried your books.

and when you got back up and went back at them
it took my breath away.
i was seeing for the first time ever, that
even though you may be afraid to stand up for yourself,
there are others in this world who will fight for you.

you may have felt alone, but i was
always with you. rooting for you.
your pain was my pain
your victories, i shared them.

we were part of many moments, you and i.
you, the outspoken warrior, and i
your silent cheerleader.

equal

this aching pain that we all feel,
what should band us together
            divides us
like greedy cats
out for ourselves,
one eye over each shoulder

hiding in caves,
swimming in the open lakes
and rivers

could we pretend
for a minute
that matches worked like memory

that we are happy
for one another
as we move on

running wild
through the woods behind our houses
in the middle of the night

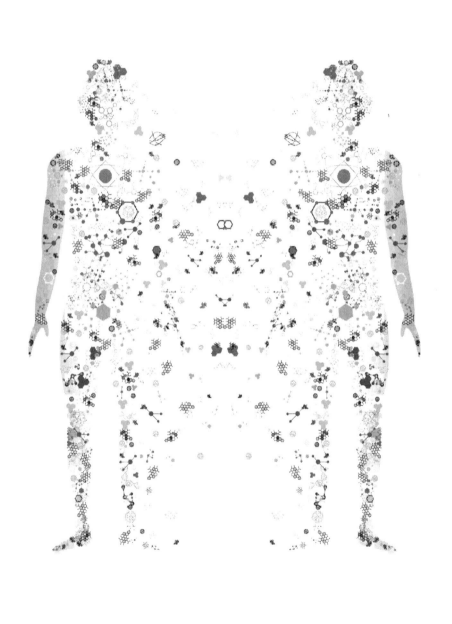

chemistry

when we were in the ninth grade
i had the biggest crush on you.
the boy with the too-long hair that fell in front of cat-like eyes.
the one who used to be playful and touch me
when no one else was looking.

an arm push here,
a rib-tickle there,
i knew that you were just messing with me
but my imagination took off like unbroken horses.

you slept over and we camped out watching movies in my
basement.
wrestling when we grew restless, the times when possibilities
still seemed endless and i needed to be careful about my pants.

time machine.
if i had one, i would go back and be more bold.

if i close my eyes and try hard, i swear i can still smell you,
next to me in class.

we cut open frogs together.
fished around with their insides
wasted litmus paper analyzing bases
and acids.

electrons,
electric…
you bit your bottom lip and smiled at me, gave me a cryptic
head nod.
          that playful grin that i would have
          done anything for.

one time when you weren't looking
i took a pair of small scissors and clipped a lock of your hair.
you got mad, but that's what we did

we fucked with each other.
i kept it.

saved it between two pieces of scotch tape.

        funny,
how something you hardly missed, i treasured.
like the tiny broken rubber bands from
your braces,
            which you left on our lab table one day after class,
                    i snuck those into my pocket, too.

how about that time
when we made an ice rink in my back yard.
woke up with the birds to go skating between my house and
the woods.

you stayed over all the next day and i made you grilled cheese,
shared my secret stash of reese's peanut butter cups with you.
we played house and i was high.

but mary jane,
you started seeing her on the down low
you grew up so fast and
                        left me behind.

you grew less playful,
less reckless with your affection
iced over a friendship i had cherished

and years later, i know that i

may never see you again.

we were born

we were born /
on those hot / rainy
days / when the water would
dry as soon as it hit the sidewalk /

when the sun would wink /
half out / half hidden
behind a cloud / and
rainbows ruled the sky.

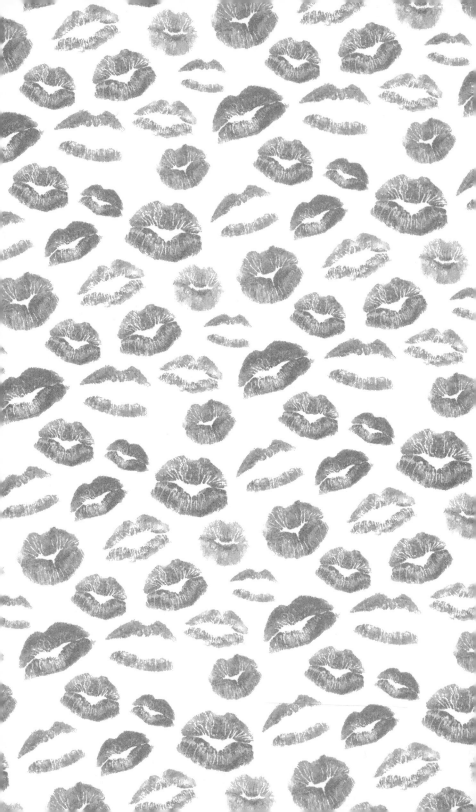

first kiss

some of us had it before algebra
or after history class.
beneath the bleachers, hidden
from the jocks having football practice.

or in the locker room after football practice
after our teammates had gone home.

some of us had it with girls that would
later hate us
and ruin our lives to make themselves feel better.

we had it with boys that would break our hearts
or that we would go on to love forever.
with faces that have grown fuzzy
and ones that we will never forget.

we had them with friends that were
light-years ahead of their time,
that did it to help us when no one else would.
or because they were curious
or because they fucking felt like it and had
nothing better to do.

we had it in the park surrounded by ducks
in the back of a car, our faces lit by white streetlamps
that flickered when our lips touched.

each one of us remembers that
                    ~ hesitation ~

before we leaned in, knowing that this was what we had always
wanted
since before we could remember.
wondering if it would change what we thought we knew
about ourselves.

we were surprised by the way his stubble felt on our cheeks
and how soft his lips were.
surprised by the way the world didn't end afterward
and how for the first time,

we felt alive.

tattletale

took a chance and told him
hoping he might mirror how i feel.

if you don't want to be friends with me
anymore, i understand.

no, don't do that to yourself,
i'm glad you told me, he said.

i needed to tell someone
and he seemed to be okay with it.

later, after closing my pre-calc textbook,
beneath my blankets—frightened
in bed, i texted him,

thank you.

don't sweat it yo.

~

he told other people anyway.

dead together

we can be dead together.
let's be dead together.

we can walk in the autumn woods
find a spot beneath the withered leaves,
bullied, pushed around by the wind
and pull up worms from the cool dirt.

we can dig together, enough together
to crawl inside the earth and cover each other
and be dead together.

making not a sound
as if true silence is possible.

just the two of us
lying in our shallow grave together
side overlapping side, breathing
and no one will ever know.

i'll be your arthur rimbaud

i'll be your arthur rimbaud,
you be my paul verlaine.
i'll rescue you from disillusion
distract you from your pain.

we'll scandalize the time together
immortalize the like in verse
as others struggle to make sense of us
be our love blessing or curse?

blessing—far too pure a word
we are haggard, worldly, denied
and curse—far too misguided to say
this is something true and of pride.

our life will be a fairytale
echoed through history in the sands
and still, you'll draw a gun on me
wound me through heart and hand.

i'll be your arthur rimbaud,
you be my paul verlaine
i'll write for you and you'll ride for me
and one day we will meet again.

birthday wishes

some boys wished for bicycles
puppy dogs
baseball tickets.

some wished for the cake inside
to be either chocolate or vanilla.

usually, every year their wishes
were different.
but not ours.

tell me, how many wishes we wasted
wishing for the same thing
year after year
after year?

we wished for
a hand to hold
that belonged to a boy
that was there for us.

for someone who understood how we felt
for what all the other boys seemed
to have.

lips to kiss
and a solid reason to be nervous.
for butterflies.
and for someone who would make us
feel like this was all worth it.

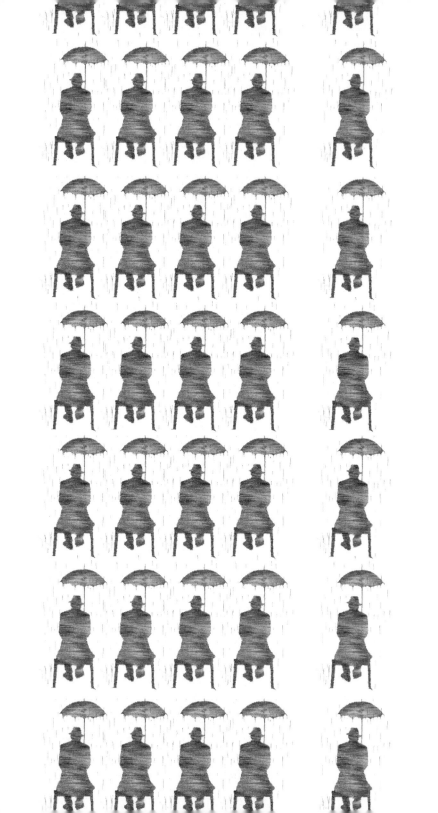

magic pill

would you take that magic pill if you could?

if it were offered to you by some genius scientist
who had figured it all out

yes,
right away you might say.
at some point, when we were
little, i am willing to bet
we all wished for some
elixir

a remedy that would fix us back
when we believed we were broken.

we would be silly not to
hope for something.

pain,
the well of strength.

would losing it leave us weak?
rob us of our compassion,
our ability to understand
why it is important to be
kind?

it is an honest question:
would you take that pill if you could?

celebrations in silence

my first kiss,
caught
off guard.

dates that i was excited about
that went well.

the supreme court's ruling
in favor of gay marriage.

my poem 'big gay lottery'
getting accepted for publication in lavender review.

the happiest moments slipping away
quietly. robbed of rejoice
reveling just myself.

but there were still sounds
to the silence.

the park had birds.
from my bed i watched people
who had their shit a little more together than me
party in the streets of washington.

and into the pillows, the
*thump*thunk*thump*
as i kicked and screamed inside, and flung
my arms about wildly, excited!

future

the future is coming
like a shattered building
thick with smog,
whether you like it or not.

only it will not kill you
it will carry you,
like a surfer on a wave, into tomorrow.

broken love says, fuck fear.
hard like a dick, and emotional.
it can erase history and blind tongues.
turn scared little boys into hit men.

tear apart your journal pages,
de-cloak those rainbow coats
and feed your horses.

restless, stay restless and
reckless, stay reckless
whatever you do.

step out into that smog
and breathe that shit in.

the vault

the other man in the room thinks he knows me
thinks he's undressed my mind naked with his eyes

...stripped away all the outer layers so that he sees me
but he don't know shit

those were just the layers that i'd
put up n meant to have stripped away
i hide who i really am much deeper
that part of me
is vaulted off like a fucking td bank

the boy from across the room
has been eyeing me, spent
the last half hour undressing me
with his eyes n listening to his ipod

when i look up at him
he looks down at his notebook n
it's him i want to tell my secrets to

same vault
i'd know that look anywhere
n i'll bet he has the same
guarded secrets, too

think

think of how lucky you are
for the apps that come with a smartphone.
the ones you snuck onto before you were 18.
the ones you open when no one is looking
over your shoulder.

think of how much safer you are,
arm yourself with knowledge
and research.
while others bury themselves in social media
open a fucking book and breathe in the pages
that will keep the virus out of you
and your negativity alive.

think of how unhappy you are
at your lowest moments,
put your feet in the footprints
that were left behind for you to follow.
stray from them wherever you will,
but know that they are always there for you,
night owl lights pointing toward salvation.

think of how happy you are
when he reaches for your hand
and makes no attempt to hide it.
how music moves your gay blood,
the epic rush of passion
of confidence,
and smile.

makeup

we are
all made
  of rainbow
  quilts.

        patches of
        blues and

    greens, purples
    and reds. sewn
      together, held
        thread
        by
       thread.

 stained by
one another,

     worn
     thin

        in all the
        wrong places.

  folded
  and
  hidden

    in the depths
    of closets,

       strung out
       on flagpoles

    and soaring
    with the wind.

    @gaypoetry

not gay at all

i am not gay, he said.
we were, of course, laying naked
together in bed.
perhaps he had some sort of
memory disorder,
had already forgotten where his mouth had been
and what we had just done.

oh, i know you aren't, i said, wrapping my arm
around his waist,
poking my pinky finger into his belly button.

he leaned into me then
and we went on to do more things together
that were not gay at all.

ten

nine
eight
        we slept together on the first date.

seven
six
five
        i was just another nameless guy.

four
three
two
        i got the best of you.

one
none
        and done

screwed me, i screwed you, too.

big gay lottery

there is such a thing called the big gay lottery,
a game with odds that are not in your favor
but are by no means unbeatable.

what is tricky, though
is that this lottery is two-stepped
and while winning half the lottery is, in itself,
entirely wonderful

it is the ones who obtain both parts
who are the true big gay lottery winners.

the big gay lottery is not sanctioned by
anyone, and it is free to play.
the only entry fee is liking other dudes.

in order to win the big gay lottery
one boy (assuming, of course, that he has
paid his entry fee)

must have...in no particular order:

1. a loving, supportive family that is accepting

and

2. a boyfriend to share his life with

what they said

what dad said:

i don't understand.

what mom said:

we will never accept it.

just be white

nah, i don't buy that it's really not a choice, he said to me.

not this again, i thought.

and why not? i said.

cause there aint nothin' gay in nature. ya don't see no two dude squirrels runnin' n humpin' each other n shit.

i had my work cut out for me on this one. we were sitting on the front porch of his grandfather's old house, smoking hookah and spitting smoky spit over the railing into the yard. the sounds of an old radio crept out from a cracked window, drew us back into a time when neither of us could have walked down the street our true selves.

you of all people should understand, i said.

fuck's that supposed to mean?

it'd be like me asking you to just be white.

he pulled hard at the hookah hose, held the smoke in and let it out with a thoughtful sigh. i surprised myself, the right words never come at the right time. it was a metaphor i'd usually miss off the cuff. the kind of thing that you think of in the car on the way home and say to yourself, man i should have said this.

aight, he said, i'll give you that.

thank you.

still don't explain why i don't see no two dude squirrels out there in the park doin' it though.

i gave him that, he passed me the hose, and we went back to listening to his grandfather's old radio.

what changes?

when a child is born
its parents wish for it to be

1. healthy

2. happy

so, along the way,
what changes?

suicide's an option

don't give me that look.
it sure as fuck is an option.
we've considered it, denounced it.
perhaps tried it.

it's always there in our back pocket.
a card we take comfort in knowing we can play at any time.
but there's also a chip on our shoulder.
a chip that whispers in our ear
every time we consider pulling that card out.

that little dirty chip chirps loud for such a little shit.
it fucking screams like a motherfucking banshee:

bitch! you missed your chance!

you've already lived through too much bullshit.
if you were going to off yourself
you should have done it before all that.

*** mandatory disclaimer ***

this poem does not endorse or make light of suicide in any way. if
you are having suicidal thoughts or impulses please speak to your
doctor or a healthcare professional immediately.

what they also said

what dad also said:

you're a very brave kid.

what mom also said:

we don't want to lose you.

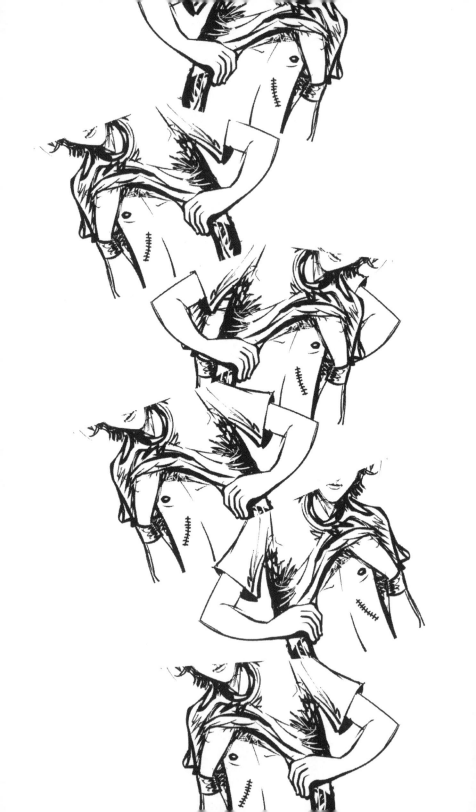

scars

we used to wear them beneath
our sweatshirts and t-shirts.
wreathes of shame and pain
before our re-births.

concealed with silence,
healed with maturity.

there was a day,
though few can pinpoint it,
when we each chose
to strip away our clothes

and strut the things
we have been stabbed,
and fought,
and have bled for.

you dreamt

i have stood
in the shadow
of the statue of liberty,
have felt the cool of her shade.

i have kissed a boy
under her cover,
felt the freedom of the sacrifices
you made.

dead descendants,
look down on the modern gay boy,
wild and free.

i feel alive when
i think of you all.

open and living
as you one day
dreamt i would be.

modern gay boy

1.
he took my hand and i went blindfolded
trusting a feeling inside
a string never before plucked   struck
in the blur of a rushed first date
that resonated as the start of something
good

2.
i would have dropped everything for you and run into the city
to rescue you from the blank faces and the sex-craved boys
offered you something you knew was genuine
something sad and sincere
imagined   you escaping into me and me acting bigger
than i was when i was with you
not afraid of the beggers on the train station platforms or the
uncertainty of the future
just terrified that i might scare you away

3.
the boy was dressed way better than me
button up under a grey sweater that did his hazel eyes well
jeans and those casual loafers that oozed confidence
we planned dinner and a horror movie
but nj transit shut down way early and we had to settle
for chocolate chip pancakes and a reservation view of the city
skyline
as i sat across from him
in that crappy diner booth
syrup stringing from his bottom lip
i searched for his foot under the table hoping

he might leave it there for me to find
later the park junkies robbed me of the moment
cackling from the dark shadows on the benches
i could not kiss him in front of them
instead i settled for back at the car
my hockey sticks and the center console getting in the way
but he didn't stop me, and i took that as a good sign
soft shy lips a little dry and chewing spearmint gum
he found my hand with his own and squeezed tight
we were comfortable after this
perhaps even friends

4.
i waited for you to call
or text
frightened of the possibility of nothing
needing something
did it mean as much to you
did you feel it too

5.
he took my words with him
called me sweet and i felt afraid that his words might be forced
would he agree to a second date
more important
would he remember me past tomorrow

6.
you never called or texted when you got back to your
dorm room in the city
like you said you would
so i went ahead and hours later

bit the bullet to see if you had made it home okay
yes you said with a smiley face emoji
thanks for dinner
my pleasure i said because it was
but the die had been cast
you said you would like to hangout again but
you had reaffirmed my doubts

7.
with all the strength i had i decided not to
text him the next day
determined that if i could maybe make it that far
i may succeed at not smothering the tiny embers
before they could catch

8.
you exercised great self-
control of your own
not texting either
what were your reasons
could i have done something
better

9.
time
and we forgot each other
think of all the miles in the world
how far away he is now
and how for one moment his mouth
pressed soft against my own.

zombies

beyond grindr and the city walkways
riddled with gum and cigarette butts
there are zombies and angels.

a ratio of forty to one,
i have done the math.
and what more…the angels
are nearly impossible to catch.

you considered yourself an angel at first,
someone just hadn't caught you yet
because you were holding out for what
you deserve.

so little by little parts of you died,
turned zombie one meaningless conversation
with a fast-approaching dead end at a time.

all patience wears thin,
so half alive, half dead,
you went to bed and settled there.

zombie sleeping with half-zombie,
angels there and gone before you could
ever touch them.

catfish

i'm a romantic and i'm fucking stupid.
what can i say?

i broke my rule of always snapchatting first
or a ten second skype video call
or a facepic with tongue out, three fingers up.

so it's my fault i fell for it.
you got me good.

i like to think of the world as
a kinder place than it is.

the world i think i live in is full of love...
the kind no one questions
the kind that people stare at
because it's so fucking beautiful.

the world i live in, though, is full of gross
weeds that anger for attention.
the kind that lure you to a bar
to laugh at you.

weeds masquerading as flowers
raping your trust
so that you will never
trust so fully again.

gay personal

(9:53 pm e.s.t.)
wanted!!
one ~~super hot~~ cute boy with good personality. it helps if you're funny and can make me laugh. somewhat sporty, kind of a nerd. must be able to hold a real conversation ~~while still looking totally hott.~~ in or out of closet doesn't matter, we'll make it work and see where things go. clean is a must, drug and disease free here, please be, too. i am 18, 5'9 and ~~160~~ 130 lbs. please be similar stats, age 18-25 (no olds!!). race doesn't matter but i have a thing for white and latino boys. no dick pics. send a facepic and kik/skype/snapchat to speed things along. no pic no reply.

(9:54 pm e.s.t.)
re: wanted!!
you looking???

(10:15 pm e.s.t.)
re: wanted!!
hey, saw youre post, very nice. 6'0 and 150lbs. not into sports much but like to run/hike. probably can make you laugh. looking for something meaningful and committed here to. have a pic? what's youre kik?

(10:27 pm e.s.t.)
re: re: wanted!!
sounds great, but what's your age?

(10:29 pm e.s.t.)
re: re: re: wanted!!
i realize i'm a little bit out of your age range but i think we would be great together. 47 but look younger. what's youre kik?

(11:17 pm e.s.t.)
re: wanted!!
you a top or bottom? fwb would be great, or nsa…you host? or car fun? 19 on prep, 5'11, 165, white, can't host but can drive to u

(12:30 am e.s.t.)
re: re: re: re: wanted!!
seriously i think that we have a lot in common. we should hang out. let's get coffee or come over and cuddle? also whats youre kik?

(1:13 am e.s.t.)
re: wanted!!
yo, what's good? netflix n chill with a 25 y/o top, can host anytime baby, just cum ova. see pic attached, 8in monsta with yo name on it boyyyyy

(2:30 am e.s.t.)
re: re: re: re: re: wanted!!
there is no need to be rude and not answer. if uninterested politely respond with "no thank you" rather than being a stuck up little prick and ignoring me all night. its no mystery as to why your on here looking for a boyfriend when you wouldn't even know a great guy if he walked up to you and said hello. send youre kik.

(8:05 am e.s.t.)
re: wanted!!
you still looking? headed back to school in a few hours. curious and str8 acting. dl and gf doesn't know. never done anything with another dude, but looking to get head before i head out, let me know

(8:27 am e.s.t.)
re: re: wanted!!
cool that you're curious, but when do you head out to school? doesn't look like we'll have enough time

(9:30 am e.s.t.)
re: re: re: re: re: re: wanted!!
youre loss! fuck off, asshole!

(12:01 pm e.s.t.)
re: wanted!!
good luck finding that unicorn, bro

(9:30 pm e.s.t.)
re: re: re: re: re: re: re: wanted!!
hey! how was youre day? :)
kik??

plan b

we do it
to each other
around and
around in
a circle
you're into him
and
he's into someone
else
stringing you along
as plan b
just in case
option a
doesn't quite
work out
plans made
pushed back
canceled outright
daily texts
little reminders that
someone else is
thinking of you
stop
as you are forgotten
you hate yourself
for falling for
it again
that belief in someone paper thin
a ghost of the dream
you are chasing

swear to never let
    yourself get
        attached
            again
                it sucks
                and
                not in a good way
    your cell phone
        vibrates
    in your pocket
                it's your b
                texting you
                because of course
            you
            are
            doing
                the
                exact
                same thing
            to
        someone
            else

one sex poem

tommy takes his hands and runs them down my chest, letting them fall so that only our lips touch.

i want more though. needy boy, that i am.

i grab his hips and pull our bodies together.

nips to nips.

belly button to belly button.

cock to cock.

"fuck," he says. and then i break the kiss.

leave him, for just a second, wanting more. because that's what we do.

he pushes me backward and i know the bed will catch me. still though, there is the panic of falling.

there's no time for talking. as much as i would like to go slow, i know that others are coming to steal him from me. but for now, the house is as empty as the sex without him is.

"you're so hot," i tell him. he never says it back.

instead, he goes down on me. my eyes close and i wish the moment would never end.

we trade places and it happens fast.

i slide up and lay next to him.

he puts his arm around me. this much, he does for me. even though, i know he needs his space after.

"i should get going," he says.

and i hold him tighter. there's always the chance he will never come back. i remember the few other times when i felt this certain.

how kyle said, "you will definitely see me again."

tommy knows how fragile i am. he knows that i would break walls and move earth for him.

"i'll text you later," he says.

and in a few hours, he does.

remember me

i could show you, with drops of rain
or pages in a library,
each rejection.

hit my head so many times
against the wall
my memory is fuzzy.

of course, you
remember me
from my time slutting around.
back when i was burning
through guys like cigarettes.

the perceived bad
outweighs the potential good
and that is all that counts.

come back to me now.
tell me our story,
who we were then
and who we are now.

remember you

i could show you,
with unfiltered journal pages,
the dreams i had for us.

how loyal,
to a fault,
i would have been to you.

of course, i
remember you,
the distinct impression of hope
when i was lost
and begging to be found.

come back to me now.
i will tell you our story,
who we were then
and who we could have been together, by now.

door hope

you sit there on a barstool waiting,
watching the guys
filter in
through the door.

and after a while that barstool
hurts your ass
but you keep it there,
eyes vigilant and glued.

because at any moment,
a big part of your future
might walk through that door.

because at any moment
the love of your life
might walk through that door
to rescue you.

counterfeit paradox

always,
with guys,
and i imagine that this is a problem girls face, too,
you have to be on guard
when they say all the right things.

handing out counterfeit dollar
bills
like lines,
so yeah, you have got to look out.

look out n
stay guarded n
maybe miss out on the real deal.

the crisp feel of truth,
       vs.
the false promises of fuckheads.

either let the defense
rest n
get clipped

or keep it up n
let him get away.

check test

if he allows you to pay,
you might have a chance
or he could be using you.

if he picks up the check,
he may be chivalrous,
may want to make you happy,
or not want to owe you anything.

if you agree to split,
who knows what that means?

↓ ☮ ♥ ☺ †

we were sitting on a hill overlooking a college lawn
watching the frat bros throwing a football around
with no shirts on and the stuck up sorority girls
sun bathing on beach towels outside the freshmen dorms.

my back was against a tree when he took my hand lazily,
began drawing on me before i took notice.

↓ he sketched on my index finger, right above my finger nail.
and when i asked him what it meant he told me to always
follow my dreams.

then he drew a ☮ sign on my middle finger delicately, again
just above my fingernail, and when i asked him about it, he
said, 'a reminder to stay peaceful.'

by now he really had my attention and the world was just us.
next thing i knew there was a little ♥ on my ring finger and i
helped him by asking, 'so i remember to love?'

he smiled then, and drew a ☺ on my pinky. i wiggled it and
his words came, 'so you always have a friend.'

i had all but forgotten about my thumb when he took it, saved
it for last, and in two quick, sloppy pen marks a † appeared.
'faith,' he said. 'have it and things will always be okay.'

little reminders of such profound things.
i never stood a chance.

u

inspire me like the
wind

delete sadness
like

a backspace button
←

are zombie pirate
treasure

unburied me
from the blankets on the bed
in my room

are a tide
that never changes

hold moon rocks
in a wink

wish upon stars
for me

know what it means
to love.

slideshow of love

on my computer there is a folder marked 'pictures.'
inside said folder there is another folder marked 'phone.'
inside this folder there is another folder with your name on it.
in this folder there are pictures of the two of us.

there are the ones of us that we took together,
where we can see ourselves falling in love.
there are the ones from your facebook and instagram that i
saved,
from another life, before i knew you.
some of them even feature other boys kissing you,
the ones who got there first.

there are the pictures of you that i took while you were
sleeping,
next to me,
hair a mess, cheeks a little red.
i promise, they aren't dirty.
there is a different folder for that.

those pictures you send when you are missing me,
the selfies we send to be playful,
to remind each other of what we have.

and then there is the folder marked 'messages,'
screenshots of the text conversations laced
with blue hearts and kissy-face emoji's.
from our first date, right up until last night,
i have been adding to it whenever i clear
the pictures off my phone to free up memory.

sometimes, before bed at night, i set this folder to
slideshow and
read until i fall asleep.

gifts

i

could tell you

so many things

about yourself

that you

do not know.

fight for you, 2

i want my life to be strung out on a rope
between two cliffs.
walking across it   with you
                                    without a net.

that's the way life has always been for us.
we've had to fight just
a little bit harder for love.

we took shit for   each other
before we even knew   each other.
from   complete strangers
from   the people who
                were closest to us.

i've   got   you now, and
you've   got   me.
each other's shotgun, arms across shoulders,
dirty smiles, whispering
inside jokes
into each other's ear during our wedding song.

the things that break most couples
band us together.
                        gypsy thieves of love in skinny jeans,
                        american eagle boxer briefs
                                    always   and
                                    every day and
                                    forever
                                                you fight for me
                                    and i forever fight for you, 2.

reasons to love you

-the messy way you eat popcorn
-the way you cover your face when you laugh
-how fast we developed inside jokes and a history to draw on
-how you bump me when we walk
-your hair
-the way you always have quarters
-how you tell me that you miss me
-how your hand feels in mine
-that you aren't afraid to hold my hand in a shopping mall
-how brave you are
-your eyes
-the way i can make you laugh
-how we say "sweet dreams" and always text good morning
-your shy smile
-"sorry, not sorry"
-how you love kids and dogs
-that you make me feel braver
-that you tell me i'm cute
-that you like football and hockey
-how you're a fox and i'm a bunny
-that you like wine
-that you like keith urban and country music
-how you want to help pay for things when we go out
-the way you call me babe
-the way you noticed i was wearing two different watches between
dates one and two
-the way you smell
-your sunglasses glasses
-how ticklish you are
-how unselfish you are in bed
-how you bounce your knee up and down during scary movies
-how you love disney movies
-how much you can eat
-the way you call me tiger
-"lemme getta buncha crunch"
-how you say you hate me when i tease you
-how good you make me feel about myself

sex video

there is no amount of time we could spend together

that would allow me to allow you to film us naked together,

and have my

face in it.

there is no amount of love we could have for each other

there is no amount of intimacy we could share

seasons in love

1.
he threw a snowball at me,
hit me on the left side between the ribs
and i fell in the snow.
let's make snow angels, he said
and so we did.

2.
blossomed like, you know…
he kissed me beneath the
trees that smelled like sex.
my mother was a florist,
so i bought him flowers on the reg.
she was cool with it at that point,
happy to live
a dream she'd always had, in a slightly different way.

3.
heat in passion, sweat, and
salt water from his skin.
my lips, his chest, then stomach, and you know…
we took trips together
and then tripped together.

4.
fell hard like, you know…
he kissed me beneath the sleeping trees
that all looked dead.
he threw a punch and hit me on the chest,
knocked me back into the leaves.
i think we should break up, he said
and so we did.

pillars

communication

~

two boys stranded,
without this
both will die.

trust

~

i either do or i do not
it is that simple.

surprise

~

anything that might make him
smile.
hit or miss.

forgiveness

~

because i do not want to
live without him
even though i know i could.

terms

loneliness,
the price to pay
for high standards.

imaginary,
the boy who can
meet them.

depression,
the result
of settling.

confused,
the boy
you settled for.

secret,
the taste of
love's kiss.

contagious,
the yawn
of pessimism.

persistence,
the need
to keep trying.

my eyes

i am strong
i am brave
i am needy
i am kind
i am a little shallow
i am complex
i am misunderstood
i am alone
i am not as alone as i think
i am happy sometimes
i am frustrated
i am loveable
i am a decent catch
i am shy around strangers
i am outgoing with the people i care for
i would do anything for a friend
i am a good alone-in-my-bedroom-dancer
i am funny
i am loyal
i am afraid
i am finally free

oxidize

from supermarket

to cleaning

out my

refrigerator…

…there was

an apple

i had

a   longer

relationship   with

than

you.

gamblers

they say that love's a cruel game
and everyone's out to win it.
gambler's at the roulette table
waiting on the dealer to spin it.

hypnotized by the go around,
the colors and the numbers, the thrill
some hit black on their first stake
while some of us never will.

you can place a bet on every number,
run in place until you collapse,
then dream those dreams that eluded you
just narrowly out of grasp.

the bouncers, they are all watching
to see how long it takes,
before you give up, go home alone,
and your spirit, like your wallet ~ breaks.

but still, you see the winners,
determination roars,
who's to say the next number up
will be someone else's and not yours?

they say that time is money,
this has never been more true,
so we gamble until we're out of it
or we hit and our dreams come true.

seesaw

now you see him.   now you don't.
now you see him.   now you don't.
now you see him.   now you don't.
now you see him.   now you don't.
now you see him.   now you don't.
now you see him.   now you don't.
now you see him.   now you don't.
now you see him.   now you don't.
now you see him.   now you don't.
now you see him.   now you don't.
now you see him.   now you don't.
now you see him.   now you don't.
now you see him.   now you don't.
now you see him.   now you don't.

     now you see him.   now you don't.
     now you see him.   now you don't.
     now you see him.   now you don't.
     now you see him.   now you don't.
     now you see him.   now you don't.
     now you see him.   now you don't.
     now you see him.   now you don't.
     now you see him.   now you don't.
     now you see him.   now you don't.
     now you see him.   now you don't.
     now you see him.   now you don't.
     now you see him.   now you don't.
     now you see him.   now you don't.
     now you see him.   now you don't.

notice me

there were days when no one spoke to you,
when you did not like yourself.
days that felt like your last days
when you could feel the end coming like
a cruel, sad joke.

there were so many missed opportunities
to flirt and to touch his arm,
to see if you could get some kind of reaction
but you never went for it,
and he never noticed you.

you would have dreams
dreams of regret that would haunt you
like ghosts of what could have been,
offering you glimpses at how your fantasy
would feel if it were real.

nightmares would turn into
daymares, which left you afraid in the hallways at school
that at any moment he may round the corner,
carrying his books under one arm,
to steal your thoughts with his free hand.

days without him turned to months,
and months, you can guess what they turned to.
he was the object of your affection,
but you never went for it.
neither did i.
and you never noticed me.

the good closet

"do not fear me," the closet said,
to the boy once long ago.
scared in the dark, the boy turned his head
and sat on the floor below.

"i am your friend," the closet spoke in
a voice that could barely be heard
"little bird, afraid and broken,
stay here until you are stirred."

and stirred he was, the little boy
to find a friend in a foe,
"you are not," he said with joy,
"the prison many know."

a coat sleeve fell upon his shoulder,
and comforted him until he was ready,
"may i stay until i am older?"
the boy asked in voice, unsteady.

"of course you may," the closet said,
opening its door just a crack,
"but once you leave, walk proudly, boy
and promise not to come back."

hopeless

give me love in its most reckless form.
unfiltered, raw
unsafe.

let it look at me
through a magnifying glass.
read the pain lines on my face—
the ones i got from
all those years making my way to you.

we are like car window glass
somehow holding it all together
no matter how hard hit
defiant

to let the pieces
fall.

cry when no one is looking.
hopeless: something
we may have felt
but never something we were.

it was never something we were.

letter to fourteen-year-old me

anthony,

some shit to know and work on:

be bold with that boy you like. you won't be friends beyond high school anyway. kiss more girls for the hell of it. leave undeniable proof of sexuality for parents to find. and when they refuse to believe it, leave more again. tell your sister, the one person in this world who you can't live without, much sooner. try harder to meet someone in college. always play safe, because being unsafe doesn't feel good enough to die over.

hug and kiss that fucking dog you tell all your secrets to because he's not going to be around forever, even tho life without him seems so far away. the future comes sooner than you think. be anything other than an english major. and if you can't talk yourself out of english, do like 5 internships so that you can actually get a job out of college. climb somewhere high and secluded and write your name so that at least you'll always have that. hold out for those high standards, but not too far out, someone has to be able to reach you.

forgive that former friend who outted you and changed the course of your life without thinking. because hanging onto that shit will make you hate yourself even more than you hate him. grudges are less destructive when they're painful memories instead of open wounds, infected. help more people for no reason.

run while you can. no, not to get away...legit just take off running because you really are in best shape of your life and when you stop to breathe, really feel it. the air pulling in and out of your lungs. inside you. in and out. breathe and fucking just be happy to be young and alive.

gay haikus

they asked me to write
some real gay haiku poems
so here are a few.

your eyes are as bright,
as a thousand shining suns,
and our future is.

our hands fit like they
were made for each other to
find one day and hold.

you remind me of
summer, and when i was young,
before sex mattered.

your heart is so pure
like something else that's also
really really pure.

i'd buy you flowers
give you chocolate boxes
but you're allergic.

i would hand you the
moon on a silver platter
but who would want that?

republicans and democrats

hush the
voice of
night
and you
shall have
true
silence.
still the
owls, and
mute the
crickets,
tie the
hands
of the
wind
and blind
the masked
raccoons.

haste
upon the
dawn
and you
shall
have true
waste.
lay down
your arms
and
do not
be
surprised
when your
words
don't stop
the
bears.

gay lizards

slowly as the writer scrawls
a little lizard homeward crawls
beneath the trees, upon the stone
his little legs make their way home.

another lizard busies still,
to welcome his friend with love that fills
their little den, cozy and warm,
where each protects the other from harm.

yet in the woods, a crow above,
hollars "feast! upon who seek this love!"
"safety is for another life
of peace, and this cruel world is strife!"

it darts from high to down below,
will not, compassion, or mercy show.
trapped now, the one fights for the chance
to once more with his lover dance.

and in death's beak, the one, he hears
a round go off, his little ears
are deafened by a shotgun's blast,
as feathers rain like showers fast.

and dead, to the ground, hard-falls the crow
at the feet of the other lizard below.

connor

cuffed
on the chin
beneath a star soaked sky
streetlights casting shadows on your face
the boy with the sweet smelling hair
and the blossoming confidence.
cold hands
i'm sorry but every first time
i touch you i give you goose bumps
and i shiver when your lips linger barley
touching mine.
do you notice how hard my heart beats?
fogged windows.
i don't know you as well as i would like to
and i never may.
i'd like to change that
arm's length held at a distance
i do what i can pressing buttons.
a word here a word there
tell me anything
stranger become less strange.
the boy who i see running toward me in the glow of brake
lights
down the road
his breath escaping in a smoke
dissipating like the night and our time together.

romeo

one day i saw sweet romeo,
so i stopped him on his way,
asked him where he was headed,
and if love would rule the day.

i followed he without him knowing,
to study and learn his trade,
and ah, what joy took romeo
at first sight where juliet lay.

yet delight, bliss, too, are fleeting,
clouds rule from up above,
as after its release from the cage
rain befalls the dove.

he took up again, his journey then,
his soles long ago worn thin,
and i thought, who if not romeo,
was ever love to win?

goodbye forever

there is
no such thing as goodbye forever.

a couple, in the back of a starbucks,
the one boy with hiv
and the other unsure of
what to do next.

there is no permanence.
not in the way they say goodbye or
in the way he's so suddenly lost
everything.

not in death,
which could mean anything
after life's light, like everything else,
vanishes.

not even the virus is permanent.
ten, thirty, a hundred years
into the future

who knows what
tomorrow will bring…

loves of our lives

the loves of our lives
held our hands to
animated disney movies.

they pushed us out of our closets,
told us that everything would be okay when it was not.

they made us wait while they were off getting high
made us wait while they were off writing poetry
while they were off kissing other boys.

they remained just long enough
to lay concrete foundations
of things that were once daydreams
and gaydreams.

they promised forever and then
ran off with our hearts
disappeared without so much as a goodbye
or a thank you for what we had given them.

left us with scars to keep
forever, instead.

they all left,
taken by life for one reason or another.
they parted as enemies,
they parted as friends,
some of them even stayed.

our fathers

some of our fathers were terrible people.
their approval came with conditions
their love with strings.

some of our fathers called us faggots
to our faces,
were as embarrassed of us as
they didn't know we were of them.

some of our fathers disowned us.
such an unnatural thing,
a parent throwing away a
child.

we may have failed to recognize
that they had a right to feel things, too,
but come on.

some of our fathers
tried hard even though they were hurting.
and we saw so much of ourselves in them
that we couldn't help
being proud of them.

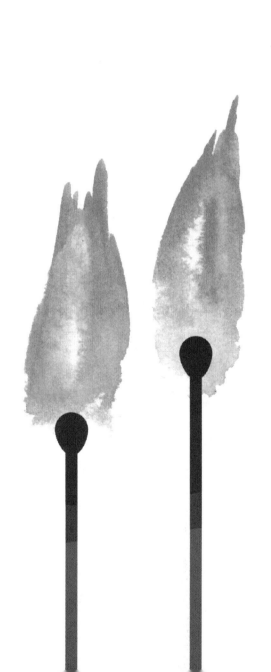

the unaccepted

hush little one.
don't make a sound.
all who wish to hold us back sleep with their ears pressed to
our door tonight.

and in the smallest of sounds that escape us
they find the greatest sadness,
because we stand for all they wish they were
and when we are together, we have all they wish they had.

let's stay quiet for as long as we can,
allow them to fall asleep.
only then can we speak freely without knowing that
our words inflict our antagonists pain.

speak little one.
speak of all your dreams, desires, and longings.
we've done our part in being kind (with our patience)
but if our voices should wake them,

justice will be served.

counter-argument

people say marriage
should only be
between a man and
a woman, just like it
is in the bible

or that they have
nothing against gay
people,
they are just doing
what the bible tells
them to do, but

they forget the
fact that
marriage preceded
the bible.

love is not oil

love is the sun
and the moon at night.
it is grass stains on the knees
of children,
a bird's song in the morning
while you drift in and out
of sleep.

love is blueberries
wild, yet reachable,
the candy you ate from your grandmother's bushes
when you knew she wasn't looking.
it is the deep breaths you take
after running.
a puppy's face and a
fireman's arms.

love is sand and wind,
leaves, both alive and dead.
it mixes with water
and is the cool lemonade made from sour lemons,
a blanket that you can go swimming in.

love is the smell of a dryer sheet,
the embers at the end of every fire.
it is a five minute coffee break
stretched six,
seven,
eight minutes,
the hand of a friend on your shoulder,
relatable,
and most importantly
unregulatable.

reminder

our

closets

lock

from

the

inside

that's so gay

when the snow rains down
like thick cotton balls
and school is canceled...

when you come home
and your mom has cooked
your favorite meal...

when you study your ass off for a test
or prepare for a big meeting at work
and you fucking crush it...

when your best friend says,
"i still love you,
even though i can't imagine
ever wanting to kiss another guy..."

when a second grade student
puts down her pencil to help
the autistic boy two desks over,
who is struggling at writing his name...

when you drop your wallet
and a stranger picks it up,
follows you for a block,
catches up with you at the next crosswalk
and says, "sir, you dropped this..."

when you order a pizza
and that shit arrives at your
front door in thirty minutes or less...

allies

refugee takers,
        saviors of
              the shattered,
  the fearless for the fearful.

broken wing tapers
    sunshine makers,
                      the family fixers.

    voices that offer hugs
  open hearts that listen.

        the humane, the loyal.
        fucking bless you.

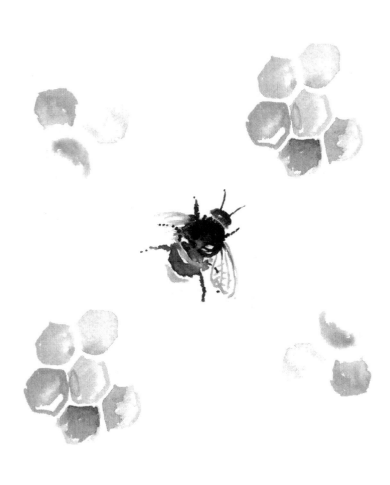

bees

	b	bold
	b	prideful
do not	b	defined by this
	b	a dreamer
	b	your own thinker
do not	b	a kool-aid drinker
	b	trustful with secrets
	b	kind to all
do not	b	blind with a closed mind
	b	confident
	b	humble
do not	b	a martyr
	b	free
	b	u

letters

kyle,

> maybe you will know
> the truth someday.

james,

> i'm sorry
> i was such a shitty friend to you.

evan,

> did you really have to
> wreck what i had with kyle?

chris,

> thanks for the kiss at the duck pond.

nic,

five minutes into that first cup of coffee, i felt like i had known
you for years. it was strange, in a good way.

rocky,

innocent and dirty, front seat of your car. thank you for my
first real kiss.

ben,

    you never thought
    i would not be available
    someday ~ #missedyourchance

kaleb,

    you never called me,
    but i never called you either.

alec,

    i'm sorry that you turned into a slut and caught hiv.
    ...really though, it made me so sad for such a long
    time.

tyler,

    and i thought i was needy.

connor,

    all i ever wanted from you was sex
    and maybe to be somewhat polite friends afterward.
    but even that
    was too much for you.

geo,

    it took a little while, but
    you believed in me when almost no other boy would.

jason

he was seven when i met him
and eight when i left him
on his own, his story unwritten
his future ahead.

he lisped,
skipped down to the office,
chased a soccer ball with a fire
that made me confident he would find his way
through the wickedness that awaited him
and that he was oblivious to.

at lunch he would quote from a spell book.
i was reading at the round table,
keeping an eye on the autistic
boy i was assigned to from afar.

i'm worried, he said to me.
why buddy?
i made a wish and said a spell to be changed into a girl.
and i thought to myself, oh lord, what do i say?

he had princess-themed pencils,
a pink backpack,
was a little chubby
and asked real questions.

like:
do you think it's possible for best friends to grow apart?

and he would be the one to notice
the few days i went to work wearing sneakers
instead of dress shoes.

i think, boys like him
will be our legacy.
less scarred at my age, they
will dance more and fear
will not hold them down as long.

how good was your memory?
i left him with these words:

never let anyone keep you
from being you.
never stop smiling.

if you were that little boy,
would you have remembered me?
and carried that message forward with you
through life?

take…and leave

take a pen to a piece of paper—
better yet, take a paintbrush to a wall…

take an ice pick and a redbull
to a mountain…

take an orphaned baby tree
to a hole about a foot deep…

take your passion and a good pair of shoes
to the wind…

take a fingerprint
to the frame of a monet painting in a museum…

take a bag of concrete and a bucket of water
to a pot hole…

take your heart, happiness, and a butter knife
to a group of strangers…

take a breath full of helium
to an empty balloon…

take your curiosity
to dark, unexplored places…

take wisdom
to an innocent child's mind…

and *leave*
your fucking mark on the world.

outlaws

to all the russian boys,
ghettoed like the jewish under hitler,
keep stealing those kisses.

hold onto one another.
outlaws, wait out the law.
someday, it will all be
better.

flash poetry

1.

> regret.
> hello, old friend.

2.

> we know each other's secrets,
> that's what makes us
> dangerous to each other.

3.

> risk it all for a kiss
> what is a kiss
> but a risk.

4.

> on our second date
> we gave each other
> our real names.

5.

> we are gay
> and poetic
> and free.

6.

> somewhere over that horizon
> _____ he _____
> waits for me.

7.

an option is hope
and hope is
everything.

8.

the hard part isn't liking boys
it's liking the right boy.

9.

what my sister said:
"aw ant, it's okay."

10.

reason to like guys:
they can be tigers one minute and kittens the
next.

11.

shout out
to all the lesbians
that will read this!

12.

have you ever seen that picture
of a cat looking into a mirror and seeing a lion?

it's how you see yourself
that defines
you.

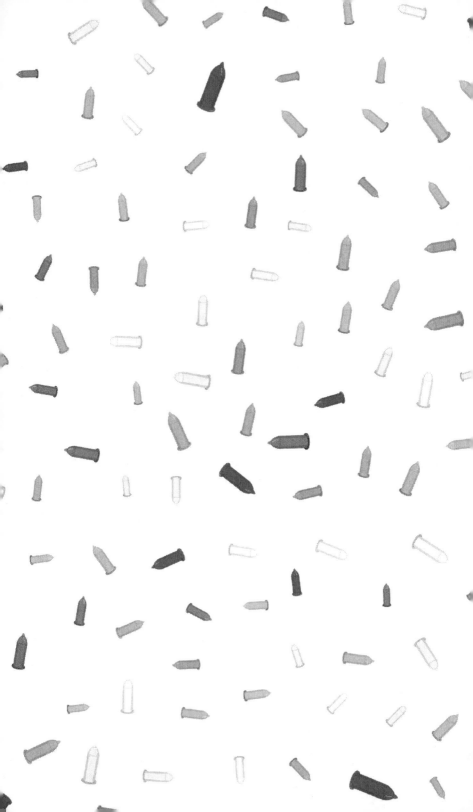

13.

i will not
be his victim.

14.

fucking
be careful
fucking.

15.

being more out than someone
does not make you
gayer than someone.
it does not make you better than someone.

16.

prep
is not a condom.

17.

he came
with no instruction manual.

18.

love lost
for no reason
…is quite stupid.

19.

never let them make you feel
small.

20.

> g ive me your everything
> a nd i will give
> y ou my everything, too.

21.

> f_ck f_ck f_ck f_ck f_ck f_ck
> f_ck f_ck f_ck f_ck f_ck f_ck
> f_ck f_ck f_ck f_ck f_ck f_ck
> ......things just aren't the same without u.

22.

> when we came out to each other
> it became our job to
> protect one another.

23.

> it is so easy
> in the heat of the moment
> to disregard your own safety.

24.

> "what the fuck is a false negative?"
> google it.

25.

> the right size matters.

26.

> kiss me like a promise kept,
> sweet and unexpected.

27.

i see the quarterback, with his dad watching,
put an arm around the shoulder of
a gay cheerleader
and i am proud of my generation.

28.

i can tell you what
heaven is in one short word:
happiness, my friend.

29.

a missed opportunity to smile
is alone a reason to frown.

30.

another reason to like guys:
their butts.

31.

boy had so many feathers in his cap
he looked like a fucking peacock.

32.

cheat
and it's deuces.

33.

personal answer:
i would not take the pill.

34.

dream gay dreams
daring and unstatic.

35.

before the bully and the faggot
had a problem, they had
playdates and sleepovers.

36.

we make things so much more difficult for each other
than they need to be.

37.

pride:
i picked my head up
and went to school like nothing was wrong.

38.

hope:
we imagine that things
will be better
someday.

39.

boy bit my neck up so bad
i started calling him edward.

40.

romance lives.

41.

and i will kiss him in the rain.
and in the dark. and on a train.
and in a car. and in a tree.

42.

stupid boy,
i would have given you the world.

43.

in a world full of text messages,
virtual happy birthdays, and pixilated 'i love yous,'
give him flowers.
slip love notes into the pockets of his jeans.

44.

afraid to get tested?
be more afraid of what that virus is doing to you, untreated.

45.

the walks we used to take together
i now take alone
and think of you.

46.

remnants of light in
the darkness. this is
how i remember you.

47.

there is still enough future ahead of me
to make up for the past.

here's to you

shout out to the ones that i've dated
the girls and the boys, both alike…
the gays, and the faggots, the bitches…
the blonde haired cheerleaders and the dykes…

the jocks locked up tight in their closets…
the flames that burn bright through the night…
the love that we had 'fore we lost it…
the happy times and the frights.

you've been great, you're the best, thanks for coming
and cumming and running away,
the romantics, the players, the drifters…
the emotional and the cliché…

cheers to the firsts bits of everything
the kisses, the sex, and the love…
the heartache that i wasn't expecting…
and the feelings i'll never be rid of.

to the *i love yous* unspoken and spoken…
to the lies and the promises, too…
to the vows that were made and then broken…
here's to you, here's to you, here's to you.

coloring crayons

he colored the yellow wrapper red
and the red one blue
and the blue one purple.

and so on
and so on
and so on
until

he could
no longer tell
which was which.

2nd grade story

once, there was a penguin.
he was lost and needed to find his way home.
he was an unhappy penguin.
because all of the kids said he could not play with them.

so he left his house and ran away.
he went to the park and rode on the swings.
he went to the zoo and saw all the other animals.
he walked to the mountains and played in all the snow.

the snow made him a little happy cause penguins like the snow.
but he was still sad.
because he was still all alone.

and then the penguin found a friend.
his friend was another penguin who had also runned away.
they played in the snow and swam in the water.
the penguin loved his friend.

but he missed his family.
his friend penguin did not have a family.
so they both wanted to go back to the first penguin's home.
but the first penguin did not know where his home was
anymore.

so they both decided to make a home on a mountain together
in the snow.
and the penguins were happy.

the end.

and so
i will leave you,
for now,
to face the world.

you are
never as alone
as you think.

never be afraid
to ask for help.

never, ever
give up.

never stop
loving life.

thank you
for your support.

— joseph anthony ♥

joseph anthony

is a twenty-something-year-old writer from new jersey. he attended rutgers university and his writing has been featured in *lavender review, scarlet leaf review, samsara, danse macabre, the corner club press,* and *five 2 one,* among others. his poem "republicans and democrats" was a winner of the *yellow chair review's* "rock the chair challenge." anthony is the author of three other books, "an uneaten breakfast: collected stories and poems"; "the alphabet of dating," a novel; and "some college somewhere," stories chronicling the life of a self-destructive college student (all available at diamondmillpress.com and on amazon). when he is not writing, anthony is busy working with grammar school students in new jersey.

if you enjoyed the book, or would like to contact joseph anthony, reach out to him by direct messaging his instagram: @gaypoetry.

acknowledgments

as always, profound thanks to kelly smith for her guidance, and for helping me get my feet under me as a writer. thanks to john martinetti of jem graphics for his continued efforts on the diamond mill press website and for having the courage to admit to me when i was younger that he, too, writes poetry, which inspires me to this day. to all the artists at shutterstock, your work is amazing. to aj, nic, james, and geovanny, who all read an early version of the book's manuscript, for your advice, feedback, and quotes. to any other writer, gay or straight, who has inspired me along the way. thanks to my followers on instagram, twitter, and tumblr, your support and encouragement helped me decide to go all in with this book and it would simply not exist without you (please spread the word about this book to your friends, if you enjoyed it). to the literary magazines who accepted and first-published many of these poems, it is an honor to share my work with your readers. to my loyal friends, of which i am blessed to have many, for standing by me and for always being there for me. special thanks to lori and ray mckee, and emma kong for being my allies from afar. and finally, thank you to my parents, louis and linda, and my sister alaina, for their support and unconditional love. ...thank you all!

believe

with

every

breath

that

you

will

find

him

Imagine if love was like fireflies.

I will not be his victim

WE ARE GAY
AND POETIC
AND FREE.

GAYPOETRY

B bold

B free

B you

For more gay poetry follow

Joseph Anthony's

 @gaypoetry

on Instagram

he had 3 arms,
if you know
what i mean.

...i put them there.

those scratch marks on
his back...

gaypoetry

Also by Joseph Anthony

An Uneaten Breakfast:
Collected Stories and Poems

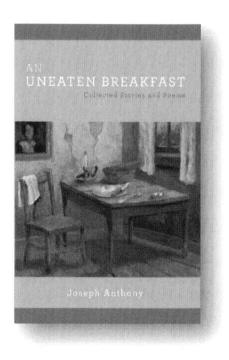

"True Love said to Destiny, "You bring out
the best in me."

* Available at → diamondmillpress.com

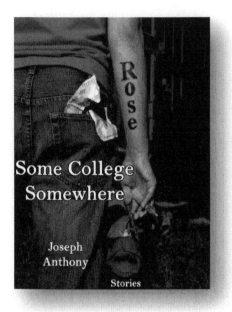

And now, a brief preview of

The Alphabet of Dating

by Joseph Anthony

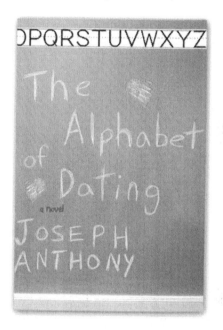

Remember your first crush, first kiss, first love? Each person holds a special place in your alphabet. We all have an Alphabet of Dating... what does *your* alphabet look like?

* Available at → diamondmillpress. com and on **Amazon**

AA

Everything feels so right when I think about your initials. *AA*. There is no one who could have come first. Whenever I was in the throes of another bad relationship, I would wonder what it might have been like, the two of us. Could my alphabet really have been that short? You were the first person to express interest in me. I remember how terrified I was when my mom came home from her PTA meeting and told me that she had been talking to your mom, had found out that you had a crush on me. That was all she said. When we are young we rely on our mothers to do our bidding, but the rest gets left up to us at some point.

In the margins of my notebooks I scrawled our initials over and over to see how they would fit. Then, I would steal peaks over your shoulder to see if you were doing the same.

We were fifth graders, ten-year-olds.

I never asked you out because I was a scared little boy, intimidated by you, and not yet comfortable in my own skin. We went through grade school seeing each other in the occasional classes we shared, and I couldn't help feeling closer to you than we really were.

It always made me a little sad to see you, to think about what we might have missed out on.

How have you been?

AB

It's so hard to recover from a disappointing first impression. A random bit of unfortunate luck ruined your chance from the start.

Traffic had kept you from getting to the Starbucks on time, but that wasn't it.

You had texted me to let me know that you were running late, that you would be there at 6:15 instead of 6:00. So I took a seat in an armchair by the window and people-watched while I waited.

No free parking spots made you more than fifteen minutes late, but that wasn't it either.

Your unfortunate luck happened at precisely 6:23, when someone who looked an awful lot like you walked into the café a few minutes after you said you would be there.

AB

It wasn't just that this person walked into Starbucks looking a lot like you. This person came in, sat down at the first available table without ordering, and began texting.

I looked down at my phone and waited for it to buzz.

Nothing.

So I went back to your dating profile and compared the person texting at the table by the door against your pictures. It took a moment, but it was clear that I was more attracted to this new person than I was to you. Two minutes later, you walked in looking like a duller, less shiny version of the person I had mistaken for you.

Maybe the moral of the story is to make sure to be on time. Or perhaps it's just a simple reminder that luck always plays its part.

AB

And yet, you still had a chance.

We ordered our drinks, crossed the street, and headed for the park outside. The bench we chose to sit on had a clear view of the playground, and I commented that there were a lot of kids running around.

"I hate kids," you said.

I have always loved kids.

AB

I'll admit, it impressed me when you mentioned you had a pilot's license.

At the end of the date, however, when you told me to text you later as we hugged goodbye, I said I would, knowing I wouldn't.

B

BR

You were the one I told my mother I was dating when I wasn't. You ran in the popular-kid circle, just outside of my almost-popular-kid circle.

"Are you seeing anyone?"

"No, Mom."

"Why not? I don't want you to end up like Uncle Raymond."

"I'm not going to end up like Uncle Raymond."

"You're in high school now. You should be dating. Is that what you want? To end up alone?"

After months of this, she wore me down.

Eventually when she asked, I said: "Yes," and threw out your name.

BR

From then on, I no longer had to hear *Are you seeing anyone?* but your name led to a whole mess of other questions.

Of course, I felt guilty. There were no notebooks with your initials scribbled next to mine. I told her what little I knew about you, filling in the missing pieces with my imagination.

BR

Beneath my bed there is a shoebox with a teddy bear in it, because my mother insisted that I buy you a souvenir on our spring vacation. So reluctantly, I picked out a stuffed bear wearing a rainbow tie-dye shirt, and paid for it with money I had earned mowing lawns the previous summer. Our first day back at school, after the break was over, I told her that I had given it to you and that you loved it.

She had no reason to believe otherwise.

Don't ask me why but I've kept it all these years, found myself unable to throw it away. It's so old, yet still brand new. A silent symbol of something that never was.

BR

When I got tired of pretending, when I was more worn down by the questions than ever, I had you break up with me.

If anyone ever asks, it was because you *no longer felt the same way about me.*

That afternoon, after school, I feigned depression as best I could, kept my head down and tried to think about the dog we had to put to sleep when I was seven years old.

"Do you want to go out in the street and play catch?" my dad asked—imagining, I'll bet, that he was helping me through something monumental in my life.

That was my first break up.

C

CD

It was the silliest thing I'd ever done, until I did it. All I had to go on though was that you liked manga art and tennis. And since I had no idea as to what manga art was, I chose tennis even though I'd never played before.

```
Me: We should play tennis
You: Okay, when?
Me: At the park...Tomorrow night if
    you're free?
You: That could work
Me: Is seven good?
You: Should be, but I've got to warn
     you, I'm pretty good
```

As soon as we stopped texting, I jumped in the car and headed to the mall, where I bought a cheap racket—on clearance, because I wasn't sure how long you would last. Later the next night, as you pulled into the park, I was still pulling the shrink wrap off the handle as you killed the engine.

Your headband said you meant business.

Your game, however, was lacking.

I won the first two games easily, carried you the rest of the way by sending balls into the net and claiming that you had more stamina than me. It clearly meant more to you, and although I wanted to win, losing seemed like a necessary sacrifice.

It went all the way to love.

"Forty-Love," you called out the score.

That's where I started trying. I fought back to tie it. Made you say, "Deuce."

Your serve.

No ace up your sleeve.

I returned it—relying on you to get the ball back to my side of the court before I could send it long and give you the deciding game.

But you spiked it. Sent it by me before I had the chance to throw the last point.

Afterward, while we sat cross-legged with our backs against the chain-link fence, sipping Gatorade, you said, "I think you let me win."

I argued, but only a little.

CD

The plan was to the head to 7-Eleven to buy Slurpees before walking around the park. It was the perfect autumn night, just before the clocks fell back and the trees got naked.

"So how long did you say you've lived in town?"

"I moved here about a month ago, don't know many people. I have one friend who has been trying to show me around. He and I went to the zoo today and I rode the flying fox."

Even though I wanted to ask about your friend, who he was, how you knew him, I knew it was too soon. "Have you ever seen the skyline?"

"No."

At the next light I made a left, swung up the S-turns that headed toward the reservation.

I still owe you that Slurpee.

CD

The South Orange reservation is home to night joggers, whitetail deer, and people hooking up in cars under the discretion of darkness. Even the police turn a blind eye because who wants to see all that? You can park your car near the woods, walk up onto a platform that stands above a valley, God knows how many feet below, and only a small stone wall separates you from the plunge. There are trees in this valley, tall and proud with branches that hide the skyline in the spring and summer, reluctantly reveal pieces of it in autumn, and proudly show it through their bare sticks in the cold winter months.

"Shit. There's still too many leaves on the trees," I said. "You can usually see all of the buildings perfectly."

"No, this is still amazing."

"Somewhere over there is the Empire State Building." I gestured toward the left, pointed at the treetops, cursing them to myself. "There it is! No, wait. That's the Chrysler building."

"Cool," you said, expectantly, guessing what my plan was.

Just then, headlights lit up the gravel road, a car pulled up, parked by a picnic table, and from it limped an old man with a cane.

Foiled.

"On September 11th, my sister and I came here with our mom and we could see the black smoke rising up into the sky."

You were half impressed, half disappointed that I hadn't made a move sooner. Even in the dark, disappointment is visible on a face.

"Let's go get that Slurpee."

We made our way back to the car.

CD

As I was driving toward 7-Eleven, I remembered something, pulled down a dead-end side street at the top of a hill that stood a few hundred feet higher than the reservation.

"I'm kidnapping you."

I put the car in park, we both got out, and I pointed back at the New York City skyline, now visible off and on between the houses on the street.

"Whoa," your mouth fell open.

I don't remember my first time looking at it—it is confounding, the splendid things we take for granted because we are so close to them, how when things are far away we seem to appreciate them more. I trust that you will always remember your first time, and, if I'm lucky, you will maybe think of me.

"You can see the way the world curves!" you said, and I knew the sight wasn't lost on you. "This is utterly amazing."

That's when I made my move.

CD

You can tell so much from a kiss.

Your lips were soft. Your mouth was gentle, confident, and precise.

You didn't force-feed me your tongue like so many others. In fact, you were shy about giving it. When I pulled away, I said, "I wonder how often the people in these houses see this going on."

"Probably all the time."

"'Meryl, it's happening again! We have got to move away from all this kissing,'" I joked.

"'Oh no, Mort...not again,'" you added.

"Hey, there's the Freedom Tower." I pointed at the tall, square-shaped building.

You called me a romantic, eyes cast toward the infinite lights.

CD

When we went back to the park, to pick up your car, the place was deserted. Had it been a movie, we would have seen tumbleweeds blowing by beneath the glow of the orange streetlights. The basketball courts, tennis courts, street hockey rink, racquetball courts, were all empty. Ghosts of athletes past watched us walk up the path toward the playground.

A 737 roared overhead, shook us the way fire-works give you that *pop* feeling in your throat.

"There must be an airport close by," you said.

I was more concerned with the man walking towards us, his little terrier on a leash. He gave us a nod, I waited until he got a hundred feet away before kissing you again.

"I've got one more surprise for you."

"Swings!"

We started off separately, each with our own feet dangling, scraping the dirt while we swung. Until you jumped off, landed gracefully, waited for me to slow down before jumping onto my lap and wrapping your legs around me.

We stayed like this for almost an hour. Lip-locked beneath a navy, star-soaked sky. As my pants grew tighter, I knew you could feel it, and I felt the need to say something.

"I don't know if you were expecting anything more from tonight but..." I'm not the kind of person who sleeps with someone early on if I really like them.

"What? Oh, no. I'm fine with just kissing."

"I'm sorry I ruined the mood."

"No," you said. "You didn't."

But it felt like I had.

Resting your head on my shoulder, I laced my fingers together in the small of your back. An end to the night was inevitable. We hadn't taken more than two steps back toward our cars when you slid your hand into mine and held it. It caught me off guard, made me shudder inside. I was so grateful for this gesture.

Up until then, I had always been the one who initiated that sort of thing. I couldn't bring myself to tell you that you were the first person to ever take *my* hand first. How would that have sounded?

It's always nice to take someone's hand and have them allow you to hold it. But to receive someone's, without having to ask for it, is physical proof that they want to hold your hand. That they want to be closer to you.

"Let's go back to the tennis courts," I insisted.

You didn't argue, but your look said *this is already longer than I intended to stay out tonight, so don't push it.*

CD

After stepping back between the lines on the court, I pressed my lips against yours, this time harder—more desperately than on the swings. The heat made our foreheads stick together. You slid your hands into my back pockets and we swayed there listening to the wind in the trees.

The night had come full circle.

CD

Later, just as I had gotten out of the shower and was getting ready for bed, you texted me.

> You: I had a wonderful time to-
> night...Thank you for everything

I tried to play it cool, took my time brushing my teeth before answering.

> Me: Me too :) I can't wait to see u
> again
> You: You really are a romantic
> Me: How about that skyline? :D

I climbed into bed knowing that I would either fall fast asleep or not sleep at all.

CD

Secretly, I had more selfish reasons for kissing you on the tennis courts.

Yes, I was bringing the night full circle, but what I really wanted was to be able to walk by whenever I visited the park and conjure up the image of us.

CD

"Take a picture for me." By then you had opened up to me, shown me some of your photography, and in return I showed you some of my poetry.

"What do you want me to take a picture of?"

What I really wanted to ask for were pictures of things that made you think of me. To see how you saw me through your own eyes. But I was too afraid to ask, too scared of what I might see. So instead I asked for "Two people playing tennis."

"How about a picture of two people holding hands?"

"I'd love that."

"It's settled then. I'll know the right hands when I see them."

A week later you found them. We were out to dinner on a double date with my brother and his fiancé.

"Would you all excuse me for a moment," you asked, winking at me. Instead of heading for the restroom you went back to the car and grabbed your camera. After dinner, on our way out of the restaurant, I held the door open for everyone as we left, and you lingered behind, camera ready.

Their fingers laced in the parking lot. We had our picture.

CD

Danger.

Full speed ahead.

It feels so good to get lost in the other person. Where each new thing you learn is like opening a tiny present. Going that fast can make you lose sight of yourself. Things that usually matter—school, your job, friendships, calling your mother—all take a back seat while you're riding shotgun on a ride you can influence but never fully control.

Because there is another person involved.

While you're falling that hard, it's so easy to forget that each of you only has one hand on the wheel, and you may crash at any moment.

CD

There are so many questions I will never have the answers to.

What changed?

What could I have done differently?

Was there something wrong with me?

It happened on the highway, where we went to feel a rush and alive. I had dared you to run across from one side to the other.

"Easy," you said. "Piece of cake."

The danger, after all, was only in our heads— trickery born in our own minds, nature's way of keeping us from taking risks we should not take if we do not wish to get hurt.

It was after midnight and the cars were sparse. They could be seen approaching in either direction from half a mile off. "Alright then," I said, reaching for your fingers out on the shoulder of route 280.

But you wouldn't give them to me.

Instead you pulled your arm away and took off running.

CD

All of the important things seem to come three or four words at a time.

> I like you.
> I like you, too.
> We should go out.
> You're smothering me.
> I need some space.
> Where were you?
> You make me happy.
> It's me, not you.
> Let's move in together.
> I love you.
> I don't love you.
> Let's start a family.
> I really love you.
> Will you marry me?
> Yes, I'll marry you.
> Okay, it's you.
> I cheated on you.
> I never loved you.

You're breaking my heart.
Let's still be friends.
I'll always love you.
I miss you.

So when you said, "We need to talk," I sat there with my elbow on my knee and my forehead in my palm, waiting for the four words I knew were coming next: "I've met someone else."

D

DL

Just once, I tried to have a long-distance relationship. The space between Chicago and New Jersey is well over 700 miles, but it certainly didn't feel like that far whenever we talked online or over the phone.

This is the magical thing about connections: they can shrink distances, fold maps, and wipe out oceans.

DL

Sometimes when I'm alone in my car, I think about how we used to listen to the radio over the phone together. Alternating between your music and mine, until your music began to feel like my music.

Taking turns listening over speaker-phone, until late past midnight, when one of us would fall asleep, leaving the other to ask: "Hey, are you still there?"

"Are you still...there?"

Over and over.

DL

A month in, you said, "Don't freak out, but I think I love you."

My response to this, as is often the case, changed everything.

"Really?"

There you were out on a limb, not sure about your feelings, unsure if what we had was virtual or real, but at least you had been brave enough to say it. I felt something too—albeit, not full-blown manic love—but I never even offered you a cliché, a lifeline of *And I love talking with you, too.*

A week later you told me that you had begun seeing someone in the town next to yours, and it became clear that at least part of the connection has to be physical.

The Alphabet of Dating is available at

diamondmillpress.com

barnesandnoble.com

and on Amazon.

stay gay
and poetic
and free.

68508468R00106

Made in the USA
Lexington, KY
13 October 2017